T0003506

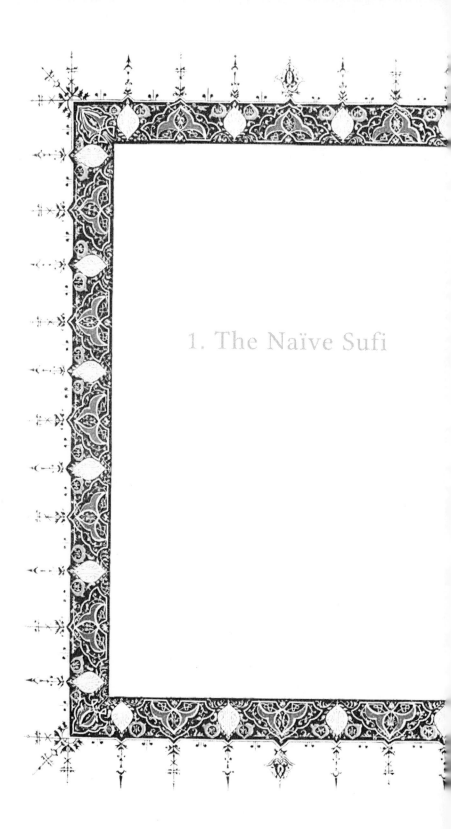

1. The Naïve Sufi

Table of Contents

Dedicated to Simon Martin Scarbrough-Wilner

I was narrowly narrator,
yet superbly so.
I wantonly resisted nothing in particular
yet superbly so
I was narrowly narrator.

— Don Mee Choi

Edited by Shane Neilson
Cover and book design by Jeremy Luke Hill
Cover image by Mehraz Karami
Proofreading by Carol Dilworth
Set in Linux Libertine
Printed on Mohawk Via Felt and bound by Arkay Design & Print

LIBRARY AND ARCHIVES CANADA CATALOGUING IN PUBLICATION

Title: WJD / by Khashayar Mohammadi ; The oceandweller / by Saeed
      Tavanaee Marvi ; translated from the Farsi by Khashayar Mohammadi.
Other titles: Oceandweller
Names: Mohammadi, Khashayar, 1994- author, translator. | Tavanaee Marvi,
      Saeed, 1983- author. | Mohammadi, Khashayar, 1994- WJD.
Description: Poems. | Two separate works bound back-to-back. | Titles from
      distinctive title pages. | Original Farsi title of Oceandweller unknown.
Identifiers: Canadiana (print) 20220247013 | Canadiana (ebook) 20220247811 |
      ISBN 9781774220702 (softcover) | ISBN 9781774220719 (PDF) | ISBN
      9781774220726 (HTML)
Classification: LCC PS8626.O4469 W53 2022 | DDC C811/.6—dc23

ONTARIO ARTS COUNCIL
CONSEIL DES ARTS DE L'ONTARIO
an Ontario government agency
un organisme du gouvernement de l'Ontario

Gordon Hill Press gratefully acknowledges the support of the Ontario Arts Council.

Gordon Hill Press respectfully acknowledges the ancestral homelands of the Attawandaron, Anishinaabe, Haudenosaunee, and Métis Peoples, and recognizes that we are situated on Treaty 3 territory, the traditional territory of Mississaugas of the Credit First Nation.

Gordon Hill Press also recognizes and supports the diverse persons who make up its community, regardless of race, age, culture, ability, ethnicity, nationality, gender identity and expression, sexual orientation, marital status, religious affiliation, and socioeconomic status.

Gordon Hill Press
130 Dublin Street North
Guelph, Ontario, Canada
N1H 4N4
ww.gordonhillpress.com

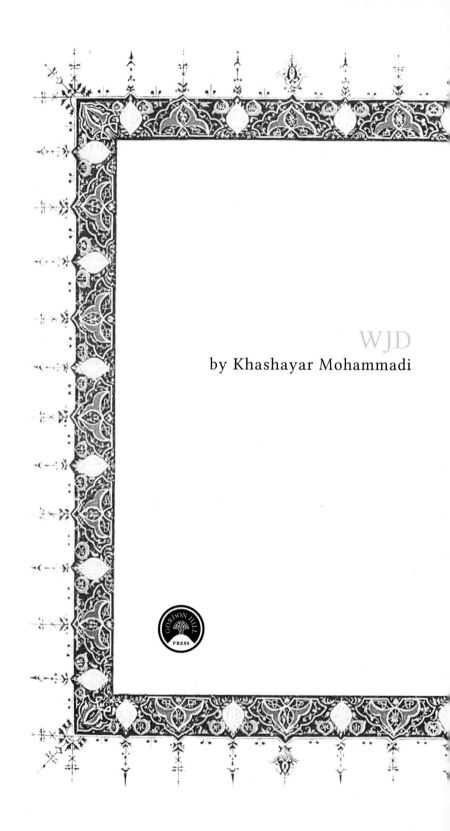

WJD

by Khashayar Mohammadi

GORDON HILL PRESS

word came:
Where are you?

smell of acacia
bushels of boxwood

word came:
Where are you?

shoulder blades fringed
by the cast iron chauffage

word came:
Where are you?

a bouquet of Narcissus
sold by street kids

word came:
Where are you?

Dad's first car
back seat
no seatbelt

word came:
How many days?

Just a few minutes
since childhood

word came:
Who are you?

a single sugar cube
dissolving on the tongue

a drifter
a hustler
a seeker

word came:
  It's been done

television static

word came:
>   *Who are you?*

an entangled presence
a mirror grown into a body

word came:
>   *It has been said before*

words scramble on the page
are mere scribbles

word came:
>   *-Illegible-*

an interruption
 a cough
a child's question

word came:
>   *Theater only exists*
>   *without an audience*

boxwood
boxthorn
violets in four colours
and that coquettish cypress
muse-hand tickling the sky

word came:
    The flight of the spirit,
    the aesthetic flight

boxwood
boxthorn
violets in four colours
the old man's newspaper in French
his head   awfully small
from here

word came:
    The face of the lawful one,
    the flight of wisdom

ball pit friendships
broken
and mended

word came:
    The face of the truthful one,
    the flight of virtue

and years past the playground
divinity become human
in the roaring of Niagara Falls

word came:
    Hafez's nightingale
    is not the one you hear

impressions
superior to the natural

Shakk
(Modulation)

word came:
Existence
has neither genus
nor differentia

the deficient
the posterior
the dependent

word came:
Describe this wine

death means
new vision

word came:
    The mystic as child

same city with
newfound eyes
new shades of red

death births the city anew
    the sphere of the human body

the small
the wretched
the chronically lonely

the filth-bliss
of sweat

the vessel
chugged
to the sediment

word came:
    Describe this wine

the ego
dissolved into
the *dhikr* of the creator

word came:
    What key better
    than the bismillah

words to summon
words to existentiate
words to situate

the self integrated
into the ontology
of the lawful one

the main square
the sheikh's sermon
"shedding earthly possession"

word came:
Even his emerald ring?

walk the desert for years
no wisdom
none yet

word came:
The desert is not for wisdom
but for clout

arrive back
at the main square
salt-crusted feet

word came:
Life
is an earthly possession

2. Hafez Displeased

"this third-world text is
a ghostly society
a disregarded unreality"

— Anahita Jamali Rad

✆ NOT

not the first to reach for the future   blood spatter

  prayer-socked feet   prostrate

books, films, paper hidden in false walls

another endangered species

  their natural habitat

lakes smothered from draught

   cities they fed

lonely neighbour with siblings, cousins, children abroad

smiles rejected in public

an entire city on the verge

a mullah   his plastic slippers

loudest words from your cousin's throat

insurance booklets, fully stamped

   shortage for grandma's pills

   tired nurse, groundskeeper, caretaker

   men who stare past your soul

not another day of mourning

leaders framed above the clock

stamp refused, another given without thought

      smile bought, smile sold

      afternoon with a single cup of Chai

wait.
there's nothing to hold the tears

withheld proclamations,   chronic
     (cancer)

faction *for the people*

[name redacted]

[name redacted]

then   a child selling bouquets of flowers

      a child
      jumping into trash cans for food

and we kept silent

❧ Turquoise

in dreams our house is no longer black/ the sky Nile blue as
promised in kindergarten, the highway doesn't cherry the thin
lace curtains with soot, it takes an entire family to seed a single
pomegranate painstakingly slow, methodical and we're friends
with salamanders, chase them through the garden through Orange
trees, Cherry trees/ in dreams we can afford nature, Dad's always
driving, hairy hands on the steering wheel, I grow up on the back
seat watching tea farms and wind turbines/ in dreams we're always
in the car on the road stuck in traffic eating takeout, Dad finally
mentions Grandpa, I hide behind a pillar, lean onto chalk carvings
of fleur-de lys/ if I dream long enough we're leaving again, waiting
for airport taxis sorting out visas, grandma smokes Isfand wearing
black since Grandpa died/ if I dream long enough, tears aren't for
the grave but for the tyranny of geographies/ the streets are filled
with stray cats again, licking themselves under mulberry trees/
if I dream long enough, culture becomes ancient/ I'll miss the
exhaustion the traffic the cruelty of smog-suffocated passersby, cars
honk behind every closed door, motorcycles roar louder than each
and every thought/ grandma's pond water: muddied, no longer
turquoise/ accordion playing in back alleys, some say for a buck,
I say for colouring our afternoons/ I don't remember Grandpa's
face/ Dad asks me how much Hafez I've read so I step out into the
city's cold, colour my life my way/ distance brought clarity to our
character in which I sketch back alleys and plastic soccer balls,
double layered/ thaw into Toronto, Montreal, Vancouver/ thaw into
train windows/ colours flashing by

∽ Manifesto

Let the pre-war memories
Let the besieged
Let rubble
Let exile

— Bahar Orang

you start a few minutes before adulthood
I am a this   am not a that
                       Mom's silhouette
between the two towers going down
axis of evil
        and at school
you pay for a death hex to topple
the great Satan America
                        not your fault yet
                        written large on the walls
                        your neighbourhood mosque

show up late to the school flag burning
                                        bored
history is not always about you
is shaped without you then and there
until left behind and done
        (missed your chance to matter)
abroad
as in far
from cause and effect
        free the poem
        from the theology
        of nationality

✒ Awakenings

1.

hung   like a this
              like a that
hanged in public
hung   like a mechanical crane
riot shields piled up   queers
hung   like limbo

we watch Mala Noche the night before you find a girlfriend
practice your masculine smile to stay alive
ten years later
I have forgotten the lynching in *Brokeback Mountain*
you've forgotten the queers
              hanging
                        (out)

2.

"give ~~me a reason to~~"
"give ~~me a reason~~"
"give ~~me a~~"
"give ~~me~~"
"give"
          paper helps
moon-bright
marble-glare
of   skin
(cooling)
          skin
needs a reason

3.

- ████████████ a girl?

- Yes ███████████ a girl.
- ██ a ██████████ girl?
- ██ a ████████ girl.
- ████████████ female?

The closet flo
or's awfully in
viting. shut t
he doors.

Wombnostalg
iabirthphobia

4.

the way birds fly.

the way your eyes
hold the way birds fly.

the way
sky fits romance.

✎ Black Mountain

fire
in waves
black and blur
scorch-mark histories
tombs pillaged for salted cadavers
a new meaning for "cured"
bullet holes in soil

        the deeper you dig
        the louder the bomb
        the anonymity of distance
        the butcher's knife
        honed and splitting
        trauma is not a life taken
        but a life-taker left behind
        (they say)
        a man-butcher with a bayonet
        not a bullet that can fly fields and
                      silence

⤳ Kooshk

something wretched about how autumn sours daylight
    the kettle whistles at three separate boiling
points   three cities ago   I was miserable
in a different tongue   I feel it on cloudy days
    am hungry in a different tongue
a spoonful of medicine   delirious
past midnight   and moonlit chests
watched for each breath
              IN
                      OUT
              IN
                      OUT
              IN

                      OUT
    pillow in hand   can't wake them three
    nights in a row can I   ?
    Arshia used to say *each city's cigarettes taste of*
its people's misery
and we laughed   shared a cigarette
    and today

dried leaves
rustling

ground turned salt
(to) Fall
(to) Season

✥ A Different Breed of Human

like Saturn, the Revolution Devours its Children
— Jacques Mallet Du Pan

must have been a different breed of human   to live
by the friction in your throat
living slogan to slogan   knives
stuck in brothers' backs
marching shoulder to shoulder   and
your Mother never knew
    you were the torch that lit the first burning car

must have lived in a different world   when your
future meant raining bullets
    brutalist architecture to hold meetings
      covert operations
posters the women hid in underwear, bras, hijab
    all the places that were forbidden to look
lectures books thought   slid under doors
      smuggled and copied for all

must have been different skies   when bullets hailed
and cracked pavements
    children sleeping to single-shot executions
    (no prosecution)
if they are innocent they are martyrs   Mom
remembers when Khalkhaali came to town
on the way to school   a single back alley
with seven bullet holes
a single back alley to avoid from now on

must have been a different life   to hurry home
before curfew   go into labour
groped by army men   *just making*
sure

must have been a different breed
screaming freedom into gun barrels
carrying dead brothers to sidewalks   but all
dissent breeds dissent

yesterday's iconoclasts made new idols

"Our Revolution was an explosion of Light"
new idylls   an arm for an eye

must have been a surprise   to build anew
          watch it crumble
        observe the men you upheld   kill
          and kill and kill
barrels of prison issue slippers emptied
a single day's dissidents killed and done

❧ The Odalisque

After Picasso, Ingres, Matisse and Fatema Mernissi

the first western eyes
to ever enter the harem wrote
"women were dressed in trousers
long sleeves"
described the women as "masculine"
a place of friendship
the warmth of elders
threading the youngsters' eyebrows
combing their hair
anything but a garden
or a steaming hammam
with female nakedness erect
and lips beckoning
western men dreamt of it
wrote of it
smiled when Fatema wrote
"I was born in a harem"
smiled as if
Scheherazaade accepted her fate
on the first
or second
or one thousandth night

ᗕ Peut-étant

after Edouard Glissant

I write the sea, but I don't belong
memories folding back on themselves
childhood room, cartoon sticker, red-brick wall
my clavicle crack and sugar cubes
clinking on the rim of the Chai glass
childhood: a silence between two ciphers
each wave a new solitude
but for others (I've heard)
the only belonging
to walk until one becomes
the horizon
but I am not current
am stagnant like the may-be
                    a may-fly,

a may-being

✒ The Antlered Wine-Bearer

After Alireza Shojaian's Sous le Ciel de Shiraz

say, we begin in doubt
but our consciousness
makes sense of it anyway

say, whether said or unsaid
there was but one voice speaking

say, the antler gores, accidentally healing

say, we find in Sufism a diamond
the exact width, height, and breadth
as the gap in our narrative

and so bursts the dam

when the elders drink the wine
it takes them to the natural
and I want my diamonds cheap
won't settle for less

Say: *Wine bearer! what's a unit of history?*
time dilates in the generation gap
watch me push the sky away and
bring me another

bring me another

*

empty shapes that form a firm corpus:
                              this corpulent flower
don't touch my circles and murdered
sacred lines and their proclivity towards order
or order and its tendency to sacrifice

what are you scared of?

                    all things eternal
                              like heaven
the eye watches the I
weeping on the touch screen
a room built for death
a crescent moon and dagger
judged by the skin peeled off and draped on the nightstand
rid of the eye, the poem worries about itself, judging the four
corners that echo the faintest vibration of sleep. shapes emptied
as figures swell with shadows, clinging to enlarge and enlarge and
enlarge: a pinch, or water: the darkness that reflects, retracts and
distorts: the subset as the set that contains itself.
roadside walnuts
stopping for prayer
my first urinal
sky as heatmap
sky as the mind's wallpaper
sky as ruler for distance but
where is
the home
of my
poem?

*

"to the smoke the city bowed to the smoke it is a raft of wind" — Adonis

patience in the elder's eyes that saw the movement, then its downfall. patience in eyes bloodshot from wine. we just sat and listened, "The Oceanic Feeling" BUT... *no one reads Freud anymore,* as Al Aqsa Mosque kept burning.

a fire, a glance, an agent light. which side of the eye houses the I?

the unravelling that forces a frame, the bold proclamation of fragments in the absence of the whole. a truth prosthetic to our understanding.

an object climbs into light (into being), is lit, swells with shadows, projects its being into an inflatable tail. which side of the light do I exist on? an object climbs into fire (into being), is burnt, proclaims its legacy with an annihilation so breathable. which side of the screen do I exist on?

my eyes on the hands that drop this year's hope into the election box. my eyes on the hands that collect this year's rage from the election box.

an eye births the I, so I close my eyes and play God. the unspeakable is my safest place to hide.

light as building block, mosaic to our resonance with the natural, whatever that may be. fire as building block, granular to our resonance with the fleeting, whatever that may be.

history disrupts, and I echo: a docile clenched fist in my pocket.

the broken beer, the spill's lengthening strides down the alley, stretching my whiskey-thickened thoughts into anathema.

the eyes that saw, the arms that carried, bleeding onto pavements. the eyes that begot. the eyes that forgot. the eyes and questioning. the eyes and questioning.

*

my city the city, or wherever I'm flung into the arms of back alleys
and streetcorner loot: the art of lower class feeling: to start at the
shoe. asphalt: faulted at the foundation and sinking. I neighbour a
dozen names for Allah by proximity, I build clay bowls to crush: *can
you feel the durability of the mosque?* fill the tile cracks in colour,
Kintsugi my history into pride: broken. pride the history into cities:
trodden barefoot.

and my city that isn't my city, arms stretched, cowering under
transmission towers: rain-trickling metal. not this—
I'm partial to highways, having slept next to one, roads crackling
beneath car tires is my ocean, chain-linked and separate

once my city was my city, says the history book, pointing fingers.
the "nomad' says *no city or civilization*, no organ for organization.
seeding in ancient clothing, still unsure: we watch rain roll down
the street where rivers used to be, *no city or civilization* but faith
but sky: the natural curve: a nation wounded by the notion of a
country.

my city resurrected in, a lord manifest in names I've forgotten: I'll
study you and in words I'll manifest the truthful. prophecy as death
reborn: rebirth as blossoming to flames: flame as heat, flame as
blindness. flame as blighted leaves of memory: some speak of a heat
so residual: having seen the colossus fall far too many times, the
failure to cultivate a ground bearing fruit.

> *a poetics of exile*, scribed onto the cracked bas relief of the
once-imperial
>> *a poetics of oppression* scribed in blood and up for auction
>> *a poetics of blood*, a new fetish for capital
>> *a poetics of capital*, the cracks of our history
>>> *a poetics of history: a poetics of*
exile:

fruit geography
animal geography:
regional mythology
black/ grey / white mythos
            from Khaak to Khaakestar
                        a poetics of compliance: with Rumi at
the helm, *not our Rumi NOT that man*
                                    of action? tearing through the
ego to rouse
                        a poetics of misunderstanding: poetics
of demand with no supply for solace

            —what do you seek in us?
            —inert as the line
            folds in on its
            own vowels
                        a poetics of consonants:
                        the barrier broken

who told you you were naked
and we lost the sense of the automotive:
the apparatus of a single breath on a mountaintop
                        and the cunning invention of flags
stop at the precipice of a new thought
say the word to summon the limb
say the name to resurrect body

say to situate yourself inside.

*

praise be to God, to nought, to ney
the Ni in nihilo n'ested within Neest
praise be the emptiness
the colourless light and the naked vagrant

we whisper into any unknown
name new frontiers and serenade coastlines for blessing
       our mecca is roadkill
          a coup de grace

praise be the prophecy of death: the interim
       a self in a nafas
       a breath in a naffs
       breath habbs in lungs

praise be the shackles of the body,
       the kept breath
       the subdued self

praise be the God of subsets
       the force is the Jabbr
       in Al-Gebra
       to rule:
       ticker-taped ruler

praise be the ego for lighting the path to praise

praise be the prophet, the prophets.

praise be to all, the emphatically human

*

I stand in the middle
wish to be small

some say it is death before death

have we been lied to?
a question no elder can answer

drink the tides
or let the sand dry

*

a single line to border
the arrow that Arash became
took a breath, became a nation
paradox of motion in an instant
the borders that keep out
the private ownership of thought

*

and the swollen subsides
into subsets:
      clouds
      serrated
      like bread knives

there is more to foliage than breath
or bread: the herald

my
sixth degree

associated song

*

"Who do I know other than my Father
that I speak of ancestry?" — Mehdi Akhavan Sales

the dawn suckling on my psyche
your eyes have the hunter's glow

me and you, we share a silence
so I dwell in the subscript to keep up

Greek Gods on every corner
sex toys and Plato's spawn

most await to hear the absolute
but I just want the finite to speak

I wait for a knot to untangle
as I run my hands through my Father's hair

when did *body* transition to *person*?
when did *a head* become a unit of counting?

prophets walked this earth and if not spoken to God,
I bow simply to elaborate beguiling

a Qarn, a "century" or "similitude", a crux to reflect
that single story foretold and retold

kill the fire temple! don't you know a new prophet has arisen?
send Zarathustra travelling West, may he meet Nietzsche

Cue theater rain, shake the metal sheet for thunder
a simulacrum: the oceans boiling over

*

the women behind the veil
the women beyond the veil
the women choosing the veil
the women painted by the veil
the women hiding in the veil
the women fighting for the veil
the women dancing in the veil
the women behind the veil
the women beyond the veil
the women communing in the veil
the women taking off the veil (for air)
the women behind the veil
the women beyond the veil
the women fighting for the veil
the women opposing the veil
and the loud-mouthed man

saying "We"

*

the underpass or the bus
                pressed
against the flesh of commuters
the loud roar of a motorcycle
then dozens, raining down the freeway
fear of a police patrol

we don't go out anymore
and a new prison made
of parents and parking tickets
he yelled at me
an open blouse
tried to cover me up

households
kept warm with a slap
faces melting in excuses,
a car tire slashed for held beliefs
another slashed for lost values
tires slashed for tire slashes

your generation
profits from our trauma

flags burnings at home and
flag burnings abroad

*

the heat of the cars
gloves in the glove compartment for once
sticking to the steering wheel
the *Horrm* of the leather
sightlines melting or Oases
strange men guiding your cars into parking spots
under the mulberry tree's canopy:
                    my thoughts are taller than me
and the nostalgia salesman   satellites our oppression
self-proclaimed leaders with fists raised and an ex-flag
felaan felaan felaani and whomever-it-may-concern that... no
matter
the prophecy of our ancient proximity to profound pain and
suffering
and the sun shines on
buzzing

*

I look around the eyelid
sunspots and   nebulous
news in the background
entertainment is the only truth here
hide and seek the future behind grandma's vanity table
where she sits erect and applies lipstick with eyes so regal
anachronous to the skin that stretches with the lipstick
bombs keep dropping in Grandpa's radio (older than me)
his hands on the plastic-wrapped remote

plastic fruit bowl
and chalk carvings of fleur-de-lys

plastic fruit bowl
and the tchotchkes that crown
the lace napkin ring
on the soviet fridge
        my blood pressure's high
and the box of pills
        you salt your chicken too much
organized for the whole week

*

nothing new at the limit
thoughts we stole
day of mourning
week of mourning
just my heart: the first terrorist
a single black stone to become the epicentre
soothsayer   doomsayer
hide and seek in marble what they call treasure
a pilgrimage, so candlesome to the moth
solar to its conception of love

a single call for Being
another for Becoming

*

words addressed to people
and their un-people
my madness finds no place in this world
nailing thoughts to an ocean:
     Haqq finds a way
and the point at which Mansour dissolved
the matrices of echo-located gods
of no consequence to ego

seeking words that never come
Mantiq is both Logic and
Sym + Phony   or
Con + Sonance
words fall short
so I interrupt language itself

*

        the people are unwell
say no more
        the people are unwell
pens dizzied from arguments
paper annihilates, resurrects
dominates the path to being

        the people are unwell
journalism fails
newspapers bought
        civilians dead in Pakistan
torn to wipe the mirror
        earthquake devastates province
framing the dill drying under the sun
whomever wins a landslide victory
whomever loses
        incites a riot
        businesses burn
        people are killed
        stocks fall
        stocks skyrocket
windows blocked with the world's hunger
        7 new ways to treat your husband

handwritten notes of
        selling my left kidney O+
        contact for price
while I light my morning cigarette
        the people are unwell
a single sigh on the way to work
        the people are unwell

*

I grow into my Father
who grows into a lost country
forests his beard
to fjord his heart
you can't sit here sir
and I beg him
not to

he pockets his history
to stand in the factory assembly line

✐ WJD: A Phenomenology

after the Burning of Al-Aqsa

darkness bruised and healed into dawn

to heal through nature
is to heal nature

healing at the birds' frequency
a lesson

I disobey the body to cry
the body withstanding
the body

WJD: kinesis of the soul,
my soul crashes at the base of my skull

Noor: the flames of Al-Aqsa Mosque
silhouetted bodies, dancing

maWJuD: *what makes you bodied?*
what lets lips touch what's holy?

WJD: overcome by existence
"overwhelmed" to be exact

Noor: I held hands with a tree,
watched it branch and blossom

WuJuD: I opened my eyes to paper arguments,
paper expulsion, paper genocide

WJD: the tongue circles the و Vaav و of existence
و and و

Noor: the healing touch of windows
being windowed

time dilates in the thought-span of a poem
smoke moves to the nose
words   written a few thoughts later:
fire in my lungs

DO NOT DISTURB
AM   REIFYING

        smoke break
                wine breaks
and I find out where in my body I weep
so I open a window,
am now windowed   gazed from afar
the single light on the horizon
over the lake
over the moon persevering through daylight
trying to PUSH THROUGH
this stasis
albeit the impossibility of
                        stasis

I tree my torso to branch
bone marrow the sap and
what reminds also remembers
I swim until I am the horizon
I stubbornly
    PUSH THROUGH
the endless landscape
unlearn to remember
calm down
        in waves
        in ripples
recapture the alchemy of despair

Hamsayeh: The Conumbrant

When I write "we" I mean I
When I write "I" I mean if
When I write "if" I mean yes

then the impeccable word
in a shadow

when I step out the house
I borrow my shadow,
ooze criss-crossed on cold mosaic

witching hour sunspots
supernova behind eyelids
I am ten nostrils short of a deep breath

eight corners of a room: a body,
me at its centre –
soul cemented in space, in language

❧ The Six Realms of Ibn ʿArabi: (Realm I-III)

Am I not your lord?

denied belonging at birth
spat on the earth for a lifetime of seeking
high school prayer halls smelling of feet
first queer dreams first queer thoughts
our bodies our first sins
(they tell that to Christians too)
((not as if I'm a Muslim))
(((was born one)))
((((death sentence if I don't remain one))))

bodies border the imaginary
manifest in unseeing
light, shadow and border
not as gradient
but flesh in itself
not the curve or sinew
but the light shining skin-brown
awakened to the Archangel's trumpet
the infinite   (surface)
the finite   (volume)
and the screech that strips
the *from* from God

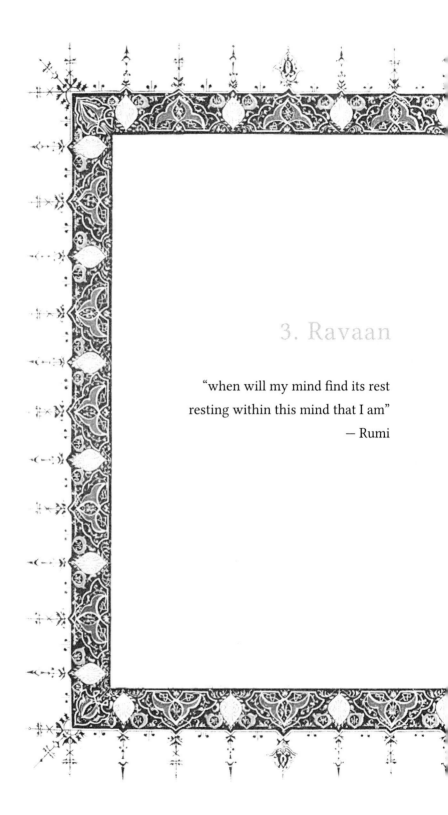

3. Ravaan

"when will my mind find its rest
resting within this mind that I am"

— Rumi

✒ Ravaan

a mind if not current
(never stepped into twice)
a mind if not frolicking
a mind if not bled
(hemispheric bridges)

a mind if static
is a mind at eternal rest

Psychotic's Prayer or the Sufi Path to Synthetic Nihilo

subliminal messages
in a thicket
of REM.
> – Samuel Strathman

words walk me to myself
      a   gap
on the verb of psychosis
between   the self
and the adjected I   breaking
the illness is made divine with the internal belief in the
pleasure of the self
     the evil is not the consciousness breaking,
   /the screen now imagined above: radiant/
the self-accepted poetry of the self is being written by the self:
   /the poet literally sinking into psychosis
realizing:
       //all is refined into pure light energy:
        /// the poet with hands over
keyboard typing: shadows form along
fingers: are gray are actually green-gray
are actually lesser perceived colours in
the natural.
        ////in echoing winds I
hear the horse of time
tessellating the armour-shell of
the self into language:
       ///// the kiss
between meaning and
teeming possibilities of
the self, of us born into
rivers, unable to unsee
the vastness of the
ocean.

when the self is broken the self stays in the self.
tomorrow the internet reader skims the brightest Royal
Blue Times New Roman article heading about the self
editing itself.

> this is tomorrow not being the same,
> this is the self not splitting because of language
> this is the self preserved on the tongue tip
> this is the self prosthetic to time
> the self is directionally blended into the I
> this is the self who stayed

where I used to part into the cycle is now the warmth of another soul
talking me down after.
where I used to part now marks where I'll always be.
where I used to part there used to be no words.
I got off where I used to part and now I'm waiting.
I got off where I used to part and now I'm self-becoming.
It was words it was words it was words that got me off that running
horse of schizo it was words that talked me off the ledge it was
wordswordswordswordswords the rhythm of the automotive

now I am so much human　　　　　　　aching
　　　　　　　draped skin　　　　　　on the nightstand
now I am these little word farms I'm raising on this tongue,
the self bursting into countless utterances
a breath is a lifetime, bristling skin into climbing out of entropy
thoughtspill/
　　　　　　　dream tongue,
language floating like the impending presence of air
the evil is not pleasure, we are augmented through kissing

the only truth of psychosis
is waking up to scribbles

I'm here writing in split-screen
                              right hand in childhood
                              picking orange blossoms
                              for thickets of memory
left hand typing
what is there to keep me from reliving childhood
cheating time to relive and relive and relive
but the language-trigger pulled and killing
language compounds interest daily

this is why I am slack-jawed and stiff-necked
it takes hours of calming to suppress the primal urge
to "self-preserve"

/schizo from schism, a duality unable to settle
like a history unable to look into mirrors
afraid of the red marble glare in the eye telling tales of
genocide
like my bedroom windows overlooking suicide
where sounds are coloured by intensity
and words linger, muddied into monotone
in this borrowed sonic space, nothing lasts longer than
a self.

each child is born on the surface of the tongue with a
single hint to life:
that taste zones have long been proven wrong

Two Centuries of Silence,
☙ or How I Became a Reliable Narrator

three generations of doubt ago maybe our Grandparents knew or
maybe they also swam in the uncertainty of their future. was it the
first mullah? or was it the second or third one on the podium? or
maybe there were no mullahs involved. maybe Rome was really
built in a day and republics are nation-states of their own that no
coup d'état or nationwide unrest can touch. but mullahs await
second comings too, the last imam as "Present" but not "manifest".
Huzur vs *Vujud*, sun-behind cloud as classic allegory of palpable
absence. other times UV light, never seen, but "Felt". heat as divine
faith in the heart of aspiring youth.

but there are tales of ancestry before and tales of the most
gloriously imperial. shah with a pomegranate flower playing "the
nation loves me, the nation loves me not" and voices diverge on
European relations. after all the youngsters love their French
clothing. an international music festival just might do. a knot at the
throat of a colony, a sunrise soon to be without the sword-wielding
male lion, the imperial emblem held dear.

and maybe two generations ago there was some dispute over some
oil and maybe Musaddiq stepped up and was a "man of the people"
and "first democratically elected" and voices keep saying "was
he really?" with liberation doves flying over the *majlis* yelling
"Coup! Coup!" as in "installed government" as in Musaddiq in
the courtroom sitting in the British Prime Minister's seat getting
yelled at by the judge. "you think I don't hear your objections? how
do you think we feel? a nation overtaken by squatters who don't
even acknowledge our objections!" as in Present but not felt like
colonialism in oil-rich Iran "no dogs or Iranians" on our own streets
as in *live free as long as it fills pockets out west* and Musaddiq taking
back our oil but let's wait another generation or two.

and maybe a generation ago our parents really saw liberty in
Islam: the youth are in basements reading Qur'an because it's just
the right colour for rebellion this year this minute you may grow

up and tell your children otherwise but this is how you arrived
at the may-be, how many generations guessed at your future to
manifest, the sunlight behind clouds, felt only as heat on the skin.
too much causes cancer. and when the flag changed Allah replaced
the sun. from *invisible but felt* to *absent but looming*. the binary of
despotism: Shahs or Mullahs.

and maybe this generation Islam's out of fashion and rebellion's
outdated and three generations of distrust land on western shores
to scream foul play at Islamic government: Christians make banners
of it marching and now your Grandma can't wear her hijab on the
streets of France even though you ran away screaming liberty.

another forced unveiling, the clouds stepping aside to manifest,
and isn't forced unveiling as cruel as the forced veiling were back
home? or the Shah's forced unveiling before. history has a knack
for repeating itself, all futures foretold in self-fulfilling prophecies
of power. the sun appearing and disappearing off the flag, like the
promise of a second coming of Mahdi.

and this generation we awaited second comings each day. 12 years
of the young pouring into the streets, killed, chased, prisoned, fake-
confessions under torture then silenced, executed. an entire nation's
dirty laundry aired on national television, the youth not heard
till dead or fled. poverty year by year, the mullahs who raped and
pillaged and piled up treasures while the lower classes disappeared
from news coverage.

nation-wide unrest and the television's tuned onto religion 24/7,
a generation made invisible by omission, voices raised to silent
screams, or screams silenced to setting suns. MOSTAFA SALIMI,
ABDULVASET DAHANI, HEDAYAT ABDOLLAHPOOR, HOSSEIN
HABIBI SHAHRI, DIAKO RASOULZADEH, SABER SHEIKH
ABDOLLAH, MOSTAFA SALEHI, NAVID AFKARI.

three more await death
MOHAMMAD RAJABI
SA'EED TAMJIDI
AMIRHOSSEIN MORADI

dear reliable narrator
after two centuries of silence
was it Islam who spoke
or was it you?

☙ Unbecoming: A Psychotic Body Without Organs

close your eyes

consider yourself pre-cosmic
pre IS and -ism
pre Cause and -cosm
    /the heat map of an eyelid
    that lightsource

think of an animal
and the majesty of their eyes

don't move
consider that there is nothing outside vision
think about it not as light and shadow
but as three-dimensional colour
that inflates to hug the shape it bleeds away from
see it for the first time
is this language?

consider your constructs
consider your reason
consider a poem as a voice that vibrates
consider the vibration as an excitation of air
hear the oscillations of air that precede words
the mechanics of a sound

hear the friction: χ χ
hear the plosion: B B

move your body
locate the process
locate where in the body you move
locate where the body moves you
locate where in your body is your body
where in your body do you feel your self
where weighs heavier,
your head? heart? throat

perhaps spine? a fingertip?
move without knowing
doubt's discomfort

meet objects for the first time
are you sure they feel how you think they feel?
reach out and touch them,
try to push through

move your body into an uncomfortable position
feel your body in tension with the world
        resist
float in this tension
interpret the tension as an endless cosmic fall in the universe
where do you situate yourself
within your body-mind
what are your dimensions in the abyss of an eyelid?
a galaxy or a particle
are you solid or nebulous?

open your eyes and consider the spectra of (UN)consciousness you
        inhabit
and consider reality as product of dualism,
body as a rejection of dualism,
mind the product of body
mind not linear, spherical
x.through body, y.through mind, z.through time

Leibniz forgot to consider
truths of delirium, unreason, absurdity

what raises me up brings me down. grounds me as mistakes
pass through like water, water passes through as history. bones
supplemented by birds that travel the length of continents, a
message in my blood for the doctor. what stops me doesn't stop the
landscape

tabi3a: what's natural: a weekend trip with the family
Mahiyya: essence: what precedes the pen is not the hand
Seresht: the essence: our culture, blood: and prosecuted
Dhaat: substance: when wronged, privilege affords good substance
Fitra: temperament: a garden, bearing fruit. a garden, baring the boot.
Khooy: character: what defines the reaction to the boot.

open your eyes

this is your unbecoming

ɕ At the Hospital

they hand me words and I nest in them. a 2mg latch between the two hemispheres. The poster tells me I'm however many percent water, is that why I'm bubbling to escape myself? Water as an unstable solution for flesh? I shave my face down to the muscles and pose for the next patient (from pati => passion: suffering)

something has ruined me. something has set my soul permanently on fire and it won't die down with a single lakeside view. something wants to birth from this sternum and the only half-accepted truth of this world is that I'll live as each and every utterance of the word *Hate* until I am a dialect

maybe this is it? the beauty under fingertips and I don't mean touch I don't mean lover I mean words typing. I mean these words under these fingers. I mean this cursor, the only presence I'll ever have on this page: erased.

I'm with you on these pages,
Patient name...
Emergency Contact...
and I'm perhaps sick and tired and a little hopeful of the sunrise. not light as in triumph I mean the real sunrise heat on skin getting tanned. I mean life off snooze button outside on the porch.

my night sours in LED light, wondering about those who were born with misdiagnosed Nirvana. a minute of companionship on the bus before fermenting streetside: a roadside bible torn for the unrequited

❧ Notes

"Turquoise" is for Erin Soros.

"Ravaan" is Farsi for "Psyche" and literally translates to "Current".

"At the Hospital" is for Roxanna Bennett.

"Two Centuries of Silence, or how I became a reliable narrator" is dedicated to Navid Afkari, executed 12th September 2020, and dedicated to an entire generation of political prisoners cruelly executed by the Islamic Republic of Iran.

"A Different breed of Human" is dedicated to all children of the 1979 revolution, devoured by what they helped build.

ᕫ Acknowledgments

Thanks to my parents Sasan and Navideh: they are so supportive it gets annoying.

Great thanks to Ali Yalcin: it'll be alright.

Thanks to Tolga Yalcin for all the support.

Great thanks to Mehraz Karami for the incredible cover illustrations.

Great thanks to Zoe Imani Sharpe and Rahat Kurd for their mentorship. You are behind my most powerful poems.

Thanks to the dozens of publications where these poems appear in several forms: *Juniper, The Bombay Review, Frond Literary, WQR2, Vallum*'s Poem of the Year contest, T*he Fiddlehead, Mizna, Carte Blanche, filling station* and *Humber Literary Review*.

Thanks to all my writer friends who are my greatest writing heroes, especially my dearest partner Terese Mason Pierre who made me believe in myself.

Thanks to the Ontario Arts Council for funding this project, and to Palimpsest Press for the recommender's grant.

Thanks to Gordon Hill Press for giving me my start and carrying me through.

As always, thanks to Jo and Shima for their poetic existence.

Thanks to all the intellectual engagement with my dear friends Claudia, Elliott and Thettis that made me grow.

Thanks to anyone who supported me by engaging with my poetry. Thanks to anyone who supported me by being there. Thanks to everyone who will read this. Thanks to everyone who will grab and never read it too (like my family). thanks to everyone in between.

ᖋ About the Author

Khashayar "Kess" Mohammadi (They/Them) is a queer, Iranian-born, Toronto-based Poet, Writer and Translator. They were shortlisted for the 2021 Austin Clarke Poetry Prize, the 2022 Arc Poem of the Year Award, and they are the winner of the 2021 Vallum Poetry Prize. They have authored four poetry chapbooks and translated two others. Their debut poetry collection, *Me, You, Then Snow*, and their second collection, *WJD*, are both available through Gordon Hill Press.

The OceanDweller
by Saeed Tavanaee Marvi

translated from the Farsi by
Khashayar Mohammadi

Edited by Shane Neilson
Cover and book design by Jeremy Luke Hill
Cover image by Mehraz Karami
Proofreading by Carol Dilworth
Set in Linux Libertine
Printed on Mohawk Via Felt and bound by Arkay Design & Print

LIBRARY AND ARCHIVES CANADA CATALOGUING IN PUBLICATION

Title: WJD / by Khashayar Mohammadi ; The oceandweller / by Saeed
    Tavanaee Marvi ; translated from the Farsi by Khashayar Mohammadi.
Other titles: Oceandweller
Names: Mohammadi, Khashayar, 1994- author, translator. | Tavanaee Marvi,
    Saeed, 1983- author. | Mohammadi, Khashayar, 1994- WJD.
Description: Poems. | Two separate works bound back-to-back. | Titles from
    distinctive title pages. | Original Farsi title of Oceandweller unknown.
Identifiers: Canadiana (print) 20220247013 | Canadiana (ebook) 20220247811 |
    ISBN 9781774220702 (softcover) | ISBN 9781774220719 (PDF) | ISBN
    9781774220726 (HTML)
Classification: LCC PS8626.O4469 W53 2022 | DDC C811/.6—dc23

ONTARIO ARTS COUNCIL
CONSEIL DES ARTS DE L'ONTARIO
an Ontario government agency
un organisme du gouvernement de l'Ontario

Gordon Hill Press gratefully acknowledges the support of the Ontario Arts Council.

Gordon Hill Press respectfully acknowledges the ancestral homelands of the Attawandaron, Anishinaabe, Haudenosaunee, and Métis Peoples, and recognizes that we are situated on Treaty 3 territory, the traditional territory of Mississaugas of the Credit First Nation.

Gordon Hill Press also recognizes and supports the diverse persons who make up its community, regardless of race, age, culture, ability, ethnicity, nationality, gender identity and expression, sexual orientation, marital status, religious affiliation, and socioeconomic status.

Gordon Hill Press
130 Dublin Street North
Guelph, Ontario, Canada
N1H 4N4 w
ww.gordonhillpress.com

৶ Table of Contents

✑ Before Beginning

I live in an OceanCruiser, with round windows
overlooking marine life. my cabin is filled with colourful
fireflies, perpetually afloat in colourful bubbles: my only
source of light.
sometimes schools of sardines swim past the window. I
find pleasure in counting.
sometimes a malicious squid suctions on to my window
for days at a time, cutting me off from the outside.
I study the origins of life here in this cabin as I cruise
Oceans of time, since I believe all things alive have once
lived in the Ocean.
I have a small laboratory with 120 elements kept safe in
test tubes. a bit of Onterium stashed in the cupboard
and a Higgs boson accelerator that I mostly use to
watch films and listen to music on. four white poplar
trees, a falcon, a pomegranate tree, a copy of *le bateau
ivre* by Rimbaud, some tropical memories, two picture
frames, two ghosts and her, the woman I love, though
soulless. I killed her many years ago, she was re-
animated but her soul never came alive. she seldom
speaks, sits on a chair under the pomegranate tree.

ᘒ Endless Corridors of Memory

I wish we could precisely locate our sorrow

(watches *Long Day's Journey into Night* on the Higgs boson
    accelerator)

every time I see her I realize I am dreaming
in Dreams I've left my own body
am floating upwards thinking
my body is made of hydrogen
my memories are made of stone

everything about her is an enigma
she does not speak
tears her cigarette in half before lighting

it's comforting to roam the empty metal
chambers of the OceanCruiser past midnight

Jabir Ibn Hayyan says
soul is all elusive material
    sulphur
mercury
        arsenic
the same matter found
on the barnacles around the window
    on metal rods around the doorway
underneath the desk   everywhere

    cutines in plant life increase oxidation and the
    concentration of fatty acids. a type of gradual
    annihilation caused by electrochemical
    phenomena. all effort to curb such erosion
    requires a coat of durable metal a coating that I
    apply daily on the soft metal

we are now approaching the dip in the continental line. here lies an
area of the ocean beginning at the outer margin of the continental
plateaux which continues its gradient at a steady 2-5 degrees
towards the Ocean floor. we must tread calm water here

the OceanCruiser shakes in the turbulent waters of the deep
the OceanDweller approaches his cabin

today   just this minute
a significant area of the deciduous forests have been destroyed
the black bear, the grey fox, the ivory-billed woodpecker
          all faint memories in the black book of the
night

          he arrives at the cabin
          sits behind his desk
          reads

I shall read aloud
from the Black Book of the Night
Book of Unrequited Loves
unreachable blossoms
black petals spread out in distant galaxies
I shall read for you
in a cabin with curtains
blackened by opium

he closes the book
talks to himself

there is no one here
the day plunges down
the year takes a dive
I seek without finding
doors open to an empty cabin
I gather scraps one by one
and continue, disembodied

these are all efforts to save
all that I love
some are already lost
but many others remain

efforts to save myself, a human
not all humanity, not this world
to save one is to save all
such that to save a bird
is to save God
such that God is alone
like me in this cabin
and we've come from loneliness
and for loneliness

I wish we could understand

I'm talking to you!
fireflies under the glass!

an Oceanic dusk
no sky
the sorrow of sunset
has set water ablaze

I walk around
among the white poplars
the pomegranate tree
has blossomed under invisible rain
you approach from the shrubs on the corner
how strange that you were never in this house with me

I open the window
you board a ship
made from pomegranate blossoms

we travel in union
we just have different names

✦ The Open Tome

my room
no
my prison
love is my prison

    in the room a female voice is heard from the
    television whispering "didn't you seek this
    prison all your life?" and then continues with
    certainty: "now these walls are real"

    the female voice stops. so does the sad
    background music. we are now in the
    OceanDweller's cabin. normal sounds of the
    cabin are heard: beakers clinking, plexiglass
    implements moving around. the sound of
    steam, the picking up and putting down of a
    book. the OceanDweller narrates the story of a
    father who has interwoven the reality of war
    with fiction

they were from a planet far far away
a planet unknown to us
they were a man and a woman
they came as saviours of light
the man did not have wings
the woman did
the woman had carried the man to this planet
to scribe inside the open tome
the open tome was our destiny
the fate of light battling darkness

    the cacophony of war: human screams
    drowning in explosions. the story continues

war had dried up all ink on the pages
every day the scripture grew pale
the man had come to once again
overwrite the chronicles of light
so light can remain
since it was only in light
that humanity was possible

the man wrote upon the opened pages
and the woman looked down upon the man
from another planet
holding two brilliant blue flowers
through a window without walls
love was a bridge between dark voids in space
invisible rings: traversed and connected
the man only thought of her
the woman only looked at him

and what is it that gnaws at your heart so?
gnaws at your bitter roots and the deadly moment that follows?
the moment of separating hands, eyes and hearts
following a deadly hesitation
the man lingered
and got lost in time

time stopped for the woman
but it kept on going for the man
war was rekindled
the man must pass Oceans of time
to arrive at the barnacled cliff

early morning
when it's time to sleep
I say to myself
"I hope I dream a pleasant dream"
but I'm haunted by nightmares
neither you nor your likeness
ever visits my dreams
strange faces, strange places
I am estranged from my own dreamscapes
I often feel I've mistaken myself for someone else
nothing is familiar, even the shape of my fingers
doubt has seeped into my being
nothing is separate from anything
borders have blurred into the all-encompassing
wherever I am can be anywhere
my memories have become encrypted
and there's no one left to remind me
of my words, mannerisms, habits or even my favorite food
I think I once heard from a radio station that
"you have tuned in to the spiritual capital of Iran"
here everything is constantly changing
streetspeoplewordsmemoriestastes
smellsroomsdreamsdayslovesshops
vicesandvirtuesfriendshipsenmities
poems
nightmares
realities

✎ The Barnacled Cliff

it wasn't me
it was the bird who said
we shall remain eternally in love

    cue music

she said: I have tired of this cabin
there is nothing real here
all is lies
nothing ever resolves
you never stand by your promises
I shall leave this place
there is life outside
there are people
but here...
the useless dolls you surround yourself with
I hate them all
I hate you
I hate this cabin
I hate myself

    sound of wind, rain and turbulent waves in the background

I went to the barnacled cliff
but she was not there
and I thought she would be
and I keep asking myself if she ever loved me
and I shall never know
it was her secret
kept forever

a chase scene. the hunter searches for a monster in the woods. a
    wolf's howl. the sound of panting, the sound of running

and they called him crazy
for his constant anticipation
and his persistent struggle
with the Predator of Youche[1]
whom he hunted for years
in the Youche region
        and an owl
overseeing the hunt
with piercing eyes

i'm pensive
that if like a boat
the world set afloat
on water[2]

we return to the OceanDweller's cabin
>   the sound of the Ocean inside the OceanCruiser
>   as it descends deeper. The OceanDweller sitting
>   in the control room. we hear the digital beeping
>   of machinery in the background

today there is no sign of the squid
so I gaze at the waters
from an Epipelagic layer[3]
no light pierces this deep
time is measured a different way
lifecycles take new meaning
I turn on the side lights
here it's always winter
water temperature
is at a constant − 1 degree

>   the side lights turn on, they sound like a
>   hydraulic arm expanding

anemones everywhere, pronolytes[4] piggyback on
waxen sea horses to remain buoyant
they move around in the Ocean with translucent bodies
they are kind beings; I sometimes think they're smiling
I don't know... at least these oblivious few appear kind

sound of a subway station. the cacophony of
passengers
subway car doors opening. the announcer says:

next station White Swans
this train goes towards celestial gates
with a demonic power

with a smoke-filled room
carrying a woman in love
at 6 am

the narrator exits the train. he is now home, in
a tall tower overlooking a golf course, and a bit
farther: the Ocean.
all is quiet. we only hear the wind and the
weather report on TV

in the evening
clouds shall be painted in turquoise
high up, from the balcony
I gaze at the endless Ocean
ships and seagulls
none will bring me back to you

it's raining
indoors all is well
the night is resting its cheeks
on the cold window
with rogue RainDweller streaks:
a memory of your hair
sublimating into rain

☙ White Swans

"welcome to White Swans Station!"
the OceanDweller gave the scientist the address
to She-of-the-blossoms. after waiting 70 days at
the barnacled cliff

I sat at the Makran[5] Coast
revising the history of sorrow in the waves:
    what if one day a single word
    unlocked the mysteries of this planet?
    eternity cum waves in hands
    a lotus flower brought
    me and Ocean
    on first name basis
    (the Ocean lonelier than us)
    (the Ocean
        the only audience
            for the black book of the night)

Turbulent waves. the man, almost drowning in
the Ocean. a Hawk nears

the Hawk appeared above, foretelling the arrival of the
beloved. I closed my eyes and said "O Hawk! I am your
brother!" /the day was half bright and I was in a cabin
with curtains blackened by opium/ and a damn squid
suctioned onto the window[6]

the OceanDweller's voice, condoling the
scientist with short, laconic words

tears, idle tears[7]
what a world of wonder
this universe of tears
remember this
I speak of your family
to be a poet is not easy
it is to be a tree without a jungle
where are the saline tears
by the water spring?
don't go gentle into the good night[8]
with its beckoning promises
　　　the ocean laughed from afar[9]
　　　　frothing teeth
　　　lips of sky

I got her address
She-of-the-blossoms
I got her address and returned

the man boards the train to meet She-of-the-blossoms. we hear the inner sounds of an old model train. he enters the dining car, sits at the same table as she. she has been living in the dining car for years. this dining car has been sitting in the station for years. other trains pass through. this train is intangible

while She-of-the-blossoms tells her story, we hear Marzie's "Diaar e bi gharaaraan". the music is very soft

she said:
come see me
when the flowers bloom

when jasmine buds from barren soil
honeybees become gateways to futures bright
a breath in rainy weather
is the Jerusalem of my poetry
how birds chirp in your eyes
how your hands shield
my livelihood from bad omens
midnight is upon us
we can meet in absolute darkness
come meet me under the tree
that bears bitter almonds

and now I have been here for more than a thousand years
and here was once a garden of eternal blossoms
and he never came

☙ Audiographs

I'm up all night
thinking of long pathways

     INT-ROOM-NIGHT
     Man and woman sitting

the night had begun
pine trees crowned
with the birds' sorrow
we sat beside another one last time
"close your eyes"
and together
we disappeared

     they close their eyes and both disappear
     travelling in time

all who travel to the White Swans
seek the rekindling of memories
at the White Swans
nothing changes
there's a wagon waiting
neither going nor coming
everything frozen in perpetual stasis
no one understands the truth of this place
since no one has ever come back
from the White Swans

     in the OceanCruiser we travel through the
     labyrinthine corridors to get to the
     OceanDweller. we hear his footsteps. his long
     robes draped over the damp, mossy interior of
     the OceanCruiser. he opens a tall, narrow door
     to the White Poplar Hall

from the middle of the silver poplar leaves, and along the crystal hall
filled with water fountains: the sweet smell of Eucalyptus

the OceanDweller is writing a manifesto of the
        seasons
wolves chase deer and the deer have little time to chew
the willow saplings and everything is in a perpetual
cycle that will undoubtedly one day stop, like
multicoloured tropical birds, expatriated into glamorous
ponds and this dynamic cycle of water and air is
eternal. in the past there was no night, only snow
melting

        her voice
        take my hand/
        somewhere in my chest/
        hurts more than ever/
        sometimes/

        back in the cabin. the man behind the room,
writing:

every time he saw the tree shed one of its larger leaves,
a part of him died. every time cold rain poured it was as
if a youngster had died without reason. I now know
that we must live, we must not relent

        he gets up, stands behind the window. while
        staring out the window:

spring rain has no earthly source
like spring butterflies
like spring birds
like the gentle scent of your hair in spring air

but the city was a very old city and we were young and
nothing was simple there, not even poverty, nor sudden
money, nor the moonlight, nor right and wrong *nor the
breathing of someone who lay beside you in the
moonlight*[10]

a sad melody fills the space
as the music fades, we hear the woman, reciting
a poem reluctantly, as if only to remember

what do the white jasmine flowers
hand to the breeze
other than the bitter scent of oblivion?

he begins writing again. he recounts the
meeting of the scientist and the observer, before
journeying to open horizons

solitude was a one-eyed man with a single rose crowning his head
as a child he was abandoned in a suburban basement
        he was raised by a fox
and scribed audiographs on surrounding walls
        songs and hymns
                sound of rain
every single "I love you" uttered
he knew every word
he handed me the sonic map of the city
and said: people will seek you
they will talk and then leave
so music can fill their absence
music must be sought!
the most beautiful are the most sorrowful
I asked "is solitude endless?"
he said "solitude and death aren't antonyms
we are a single stem with two flowers"
he gave me the rose crowning his head
solitude ended

❧ Southwest Iran, by the Iraq Border

how hard it is
to say "I love you"
with a rain-filled throat

      in the OceanCruiser. the OceanDweller speaks
of the past

blood of heresy boils
I relentlessly seek God
I am a lesser being
I'm born into platitude

once upon a time
if memory serves
my life was a celebration
filled with joy and goblets of wine
alas the Bible ran its course
as if salvation had abandoned me
that's how I buoy atop a sea of poetry
I swallowed the verdure of the sky
where the delightful pallid sprinkle of the Ocean
sometimes shifts colour from Nile blue
where daily delusions and soft whispers
(stronger than alcohol
and more resonant than your instruments)
ferment the crimson red of love

      a beat. again he speaks

and today our faces are full of sorrow
and the sun looks bitter

      and music fills the space

in the psychiatrist's office

recently she always spoke of spirits
and said in the spiritual discipline of longing
each year is a second
this is how spirits withstand long periods of yearning

      the narrator is in a room with a kitchen. a
      studio if you will. we hear the television speak
      in Tagalog. the room is quiet. the only sound is
      the television

"the TV can be a companion to talk to, the TV can talk
to you too so you won't be lonely while eating. TV isn't
all bad there are good things on TV y'know..."

      his last words echo in the empty space, as if the
      room is carried away by the wind. we return to
      the room after a short beat

she had rested her head on the kitchen window
wanted me to get used to it
I organized letters in the wind
till they were all lost

      an enigmatic tune plays. they are flying again

we had to depart
morning light pierced the trees to get to us

      sounds of war. an urban partisan war. a
soldier's last words:

we defended the city with all our might
the enemy had reached the gates
the end was near

a man in a half-destroyed room. two picture
frames hang on the wall. two dead soldiers have
fallen a few paces behind. the walls are filled
with bullet holes

there is no death here
all have been dead long before the war
like cities buried in rubble
and their unwritten histories of atrocities
these rooms are but the echoes of a wound
windows open to scorched ruins
where we witnessed much:
"I saw a lake with a woman standing beside
she fed breadcrumbs to the White Swans"

a beat. the echo heard by the man: the death-
throes of the soldier:

someone sang beside me
how strangely mild the weather is today
these walls stand solid
it'll be years till they crumble
here, on this wall, was a mirror
through which
how many combs straightened how many hairs?
how many smiles?
how many glimpses of sorrow
has this mirror captured in its memory?
nothing can retrieve that imagery
they all pour into the estuary

we will all one day fly from the window
and leave the cliff-comforting seclusion of this world behind

music. a majestic flight

☙ Under the White Poplar

the sounds of the Ocean
all sounds crash into cliffs
I recite all my poems to the Ocean

> soft music. we go inside the OceanCruiser. the
> OceanDweller walks among the white Poplars.
> we can hear the rustling of leaves. while
> walking on the dried leaves he speaks of the
> genesis of song

a flower has bloomed
dried root
> lively crown

> some reprieve. the voice changes its timbre

Asuriq[11] was the first flower on this planet; its pollen
carried by the comet Indra to the depths of this planet's
Oceans. long roots and small leaves. volcanic cycles
made the flower surface 130 million years ago.
humanity had not yet come to earth. it was the time of
birds, alone with flowers on the surface. it was then
that songs began to take form. the first song was a
dialogue between the birds and Asuriq

> the room. the television speaks in Farsi. no
sound of birds
> the poem is recited with soft music in the
background

I dreamt of you
it was spring
we were walking
you cried
there were no flowers

I said "don't worry they'll come soon
journeying to Hell isn't easy
half of us will end up there
the other half on their way back
we often meet on the road
and being dissimilar is a good thing
like the blue sky which isn't always blue"

flowers: all seasons
are the crimson of your lips
on your white shirt

      with the end of the poem, music begins. next
      act will speak of sorrow

      in the OceanCruiser. the sounds of the
      laboratory

      music. on the subject of pain

pain is the key to the human interior
the innermost recesses of the human being
can be accessed through it
a sort of freedom and liberty
pain is a unique measurement
from long ago humanity has had an intricate relationship with it
and is still struggling to unleash itself from its claw
overcoming pain shall bring about the long reign of humanity

in the street. it's raining without thunder. a
woman behind the window. her cheeks, pressed
against the glass

we awaited the downpour
I bought all tickets to disappointment
we forgot all else
bitter nights had sedimented underneath our fingernails

autumn passed. no refreshments were served
they had been reciting this story from years ago
but at this point in life, we must listen to the wind's emotions
and sometimes think of a wet street in a short poem

I grabbed the key to sunrise
my wounds, a lantern in the streets

I had several directions
to you

the sound of a creek. the sound of crickets
the chirping of crickets is paramount in the
room

mountains move towards dusk
tree branches have bowed down
to the silent hymn of a singer
behind the window
damp from rain or whatever
in some place
in some story
I follow your beautiful eyes
taken hostage by the moon
moving towards the night sky
on a boat afloat on the lake

in the OceanCruiser. the OceanDweller speaks
of human hardships

alienation is spoken in Oceanic tongues
the Ocean's language is the language of birds
and the language of birds is the language of flowers
and the language of flowers is the language of stars
and the language of stars is the language of water
and the language of water is the language of God

↶ Nocturnal Bridges

the sound of television.

the man's voice behind the phone
expensive houses on the coast
an old man (hard of hearing) guarded the complex with
modern equipment
we entered the house like spirits, without alarming
anyone
all houses were empty. no one was there
we were the only residents of that complex

the room is silent. the scratching of a record
can be heard on the gramophone. the song is
not legible

night came with shoes of acacia

we walked around
bloodied streets
seeking in darkness

we began from a place
you can imagine it was a house

it was a journey along the night
to uncharted territory

we traveled with our cigarettes
hymns on our lips
a craze inside our chest
and the night like a poem
by the poet travelling to Greece
to fight for liberty[12]

my bodily eyes saw nothing
except internal impurities
my friends were laughing:
certain impurities stick to the corners of the mouth
they said "be careful how you speak
that divine revenge annihilates"

"then forgive me since I worship God"
we laughed at darkness
and we did not fear
how many poems we sang
how many hymns we promised in those nights
today nothing remains of them but cold ash
        torn apart wrecks
like flotsam   washing up on shore

I also thought the Ocean would carry me off one day

the truth is that I loathe the Ocean
Ocean is the criminal par excellence
you don't know
and I won't recount any of it
              never

"adamant timidity is the worst of all sins"
              said Yeshua
let the green leaves grow
let them bear hefty seeds

what were we speaking of?
we digress to neon nights

"nocturnal legends are manifold
be patient and don't be forlorn
since misery is contagious
worldly pleasure
shall be your sorrow"
I testified such to the lovers of the world
how fortunate are those who live visually

I half-return to your smile
tonight
I dedicate this night to your smile
tonight
in your memory
in spring

      he opens the window. the sound of wind among
branches

now's the time for the pine's enchantment
when wind blows   orange pollen
fly off the branches

our life story is such

as if pollen
mysterious
and orange
carried by
wind to an
unknown
destination

❧ Regarding Today

    someone slowly ascending wooden stairs
    carpeted with red velvet. we hear the
    ascension throughout the poem

when I met her I was holding a star
I said "I can't love you"
she said "come identify my eye colour in this light"

the steam whistle of the steamship from
Luchino Visconti's *Death in Venice.* the
opening title music plays throughout the poem

Gustav Von Ascehnbach boards the ship to Venice like I
board the OceanCruiser to traverse the pitch-black
depths of the Ocean, travelling through memories
plagued by darkness
Gustav moves towards a new conception of beauty and
I, buoyant on planetary Oceans, seek only you as my
reasoning for poetry

as the poem ends, the song continues until
fading into the sound of a voicemail playing on
the phone speaker. a father has recorded this
before being shipped to an operation of the
Iran-Iraq war. the background noise is minimal,
only interplanetary travel noises are heard as if
crickets among a thicket of shemshad[13]

a blue lily
set ablaze in the sky
times like this
the border thins
between the Ocean
and the sky
we travel to the sky
where celestial criminals parade
we hunt
celestial crimes
traverse numerous planets
and numerous stars
face those attempting to destroy life one by one
in this play they appear under "The Dead" in the cast

tonight when you close your eyes on this vast universe
a part of it disappears forever
while other parts are manifest, delicate and fragile
so tomorrow can be a light in your eyes

I don't know how close I've come to losing you

    a sad song slowly wounds the space

✒ Where Do You Buy a Window Overlooking Blue Skies?

an interplanetary chase scene in three separate
situations
1. one person recites poetry
2. one person is seated behind us at the jetty and
speaks to us
3. a man and a woman speak of the past in a
cafe around Uranus
some interplanetary sounds. a spaceship with
plasma engine
music. before the spaceship lands someone
mysteriously recites this poem

in Alexandria dandelions levitate in the sky

darkness came   gradually
            took over all
and while leaving
some of it was left behind
                    in sunflowers

the sounds of the pier. someone sits on the jetty
and recounts

one must not feel sad for women who flee
but there is one single sorrow that irks the heart
to allow one to traverse their own path in time
and travel from past to present in solitude
but with these crashing waves
migrant birds feel sorrow in their corpus

its autumn now
days are longer than ever
we near the end of a long journey
following streaks of blood

a man and a woman converse in a cafe. we hear
their story recounted by passersby

she said: you're the last customer today
        I was about to close the cafe
        ships come here less and less every day
        this area's slowly becoming desolate
        I was contemplating leaving here
I said: you've thought long and hard
        property is expensive on newly-bought islands
        isn't it hard for you?
she said: you've always worried about such things
        I aim to change in the new city. don't worry he is also there.
I said: who? the man sitting here?
she said: correct. tell me about yourself
I said: I'm hitchhiking galaxies with some misfits. I'm
        an intergalactic award-winner!

I put the watch on the table and asked "do you remember?"
she picked up the watch to examine

she said: you've always been waiting for me but that
　　　day when I came there was only this watch and a piece
　　　of paper saying "goodbye". for some reason I didn't feel
　　　any longing. nothing felt real back then, but slowly I
　　　realized that it was true and I left this planet to start a
　　　new life, but what I want to know today is why you
　　　disappeared?

I said:　I believe time has stopped for you. do you really
　　　believe time stops? there is this story is from ages ago I
　　　no longer recall. time never stops.

✑ Me, Her, Telephone

voice behind the phone:
"phone numbers are nothing alike
but at the other end of the wire are human voices
bad days are nothing alike
oftentimes it's you who are silent.
other times the telephone"
    – Vaqif Səmədoğlu

inside the room. the man is on the phone. two
phone conversations conflate into one. in the
first we hear throngs of insects in July heat, in
the other a radio show where Sa'eed Mozaffari
speaks of Buster Keaton

grandma said the acacias have entered from the kitchen
window
acacias so white they had wedding dresses on
I said I miss the acacias
do you remember the year where tornadoes yanked an acacia
out of the ground?

on the way back from school
the gutter filled with dried acacia leaves
july rain evaporating
alas how short is the acacia's lifetime
what scent lingers
when you walk around the streets
but the sweet smell of acacia?

grandma said I couldn't enunciate words
I remember but I cannot articulate
its strange
how pain resembles words
if inspected from close range
it's as if words are constructed by pain

now all I can think of
is someone yelling "quiet"
when I'm on the phone
and how should I reply
that this is the bass line to my life
that I can't! the beat will die!
I want someone to speak of Buster Keaton to me
I want to know more about Victor Hugo
"what's the harm? you can listen too! its far better than
 my meaningless words!"

more than anything I'm indebted to the phone
            a significant portion of life's most joyful
moments
            the most eloquent sentences etched in my
memory
It was in the periphery of the phone
where I saw human disintegration
when I saw human willpower

in many ways phones resemble planets
giving meaning to long incomprehensible numbers
by virtue of existing
numbers that are each a command
in the uniform operating system of our memories
organizing sounds, images and countless more

that's why the phone receiver smells of violets

❧ The Deep Wound

inside the OceanCruiser we hear pressure
valves. buttons are pressed one by one to
equalize air pressure. the OceanDweller speaks

and God said "my warriors take refuge in me
like birds   between clefts of a mountain"

sword fighting. an ancient battle. within snowy
fjords

war starts with God and for God
but who knows which side God takes?

a scream. a throat is cut

blood fountains from the throat of humanity
and God's visage
            slowly revealed ahead

horses neigh. swords clink

there was only hatred and angst
and within the hearts of the most robust
love blazed behind bronze armour

the OceanDweller makes a fist as if possessed
by a demon

I'll show you!
you enchanting creator!

time passes, as if centuries in the blink of an
eye. in a room we hear the sound of the
television. narrator tells the OceanDweller's
tale in a different tone

from then on
every time he passed by there
his face blazed in blue flames
pressed his hands on his chest
in self condolence

a beat. music changes the atmosphere.

one day rain will wipe away all
as if chalk drawings on the wall
and the universe's psyche is prepared
for all things new

the OceanCruiser surfaces into turbulent
waves, sings the most cordial hymn

let your heart break
we're born to test our hearts
amidst the busy roads of this world

traverse Oceanic currents to the moon
kiss whomever you love without a word
love is imbibed through the small indentation on the
lips

wear a simple black shirt
hide your wings
promise eternal friendships
and leave this universe

sound of television. a man and a woman speak
in a room

man said "do you know what blight is?"
the woman was silent with her forehead on the kitchen
window, which was now numb from the cold. she liked
this. the man repeated his question and the woman
removed her head from the glass and put it somewhere
new

for a moment the sound of the television
dominates. the man answers his own question

"the wound leftover on the stem from the diseased leaf,
I mean... after the disease hits the leaf, the wound is left
on the stem."

the woman said:
"and perhaps on the roots"

❧ The Pomegranate Girl

I buried my words
under trickles of rain
amidst sparse red roses
and returned home with the stars

in the OceanCruiser. the OceanDweller walks
among the white poplars. the drip irrigation
system is on. we can hear the water clearly. a
Caratenoid[14] farm:

cellular respiration is a complex biochemical process
wherein with the influence of enzymes and the use of
oxygen, energy is provided to the live animal. cellular
respiration is a type of oxidization or instant
combustion during which the energy released is used
for vital operations in animals and plants. the cycle of
Carbon is completed thus.

sound of hydraulic arms operating on the
caratenoid farm

here, in these glass implements we farm a new strain of
caratenoids: lycopene
from the lycopene of blood we manufacture anti-
oxididants
lycopenes play important roles in such areas
in long-distance travel blood is vital

music. various ambient sounds of the room at
night: a cigarette slowly burning out in an
ashtray, the sound of dried tobacco burning,
then crickets. the weather is humid. the man
recounts something to the woman. we hear
parts of it:

the fish don't crave olives or figs
hand me those
go to the garden
you'll hear strange noises there
but don't mind them
you must carry on
one shall say "I'll kill you"
one shall say "one day you shall weep over your
footsteps"

an echo, as if spirits among the trees. the
garden of eternal blossoms

the pomegranate's heart burst
a naked girl emerged
said "water" said "bread"
there was no water or bread
she died

another pomegranate burst by the creek
the girl said "water" said "bread"
drank water and lived
the girl said
"my sister, bergamot! bow down your head!"
the bergamot knelt and the girl climbed the tree

the dark-hooded woman said "sister, what a beautiful
pendant you have"
the girl said "my dear it is only stone"
the woman yanked the pendant, threw her off the tree
the girl became a flower by the creek
the flower became a dove
the dove bled
its blood became a plane tree
and then a plank of wood
and then a horse whisperer
whispered "be calm you mute"

and alas my pearls
and alas my pearls

the woman said
"I'm bored"
"tell me another"

another place, years later, the man is sitting in a
room. we hear the TV in the background. the
man recites this poem

night is a kingdom spanning either side of my window
and my universe's heart beats with nocturnal vibrations
until the morning breeze comes
in a notebook I record marine life
in between the notebook's lines
I inspect their lives with my fingertips
in the vestigium of life cycles
where the power of flight is granted gradually
and Oceanic legends only contain
volcanic eruptions on the Ocean floor
I heard it said: "observe the birds! their wings mean
freedom
and how destructive is freedom!"
I had seen the fate of the heavens in the depths of the
Ocean

༒ The Neon MotorCycle

      rain and thunder in the background

darkness poured down
I hurried home
as if someone was waiting

      music along with the sounds of a Yamaha YZR
      500cc. with upbeat music neon light awakes
      from its corpus as if a soul hovering atop a
      body, and begins to tail the neon motorcycle
      along the streets filled with neon signs;
      becoming a neon chevalier

in a road
beside a yellow dandelion field
a red car   a blue car
dusk bordering on night
the night is about to begin
a humid neon night

      music fades into a song broadcast on TV. the
      song fades into a TV reporter. we are in a room

how sorrowful is the nocturnal world
if you've ever experienced a solemn sunset
or ever thought of a swamp enveloped by fog
and if you have ever fearlessly thought
of leaving such a world with its foggy swamps behind
                you'll know
that a true lover is one who shares
the beloved's destiny

music in the background. on the motorcycle.
these words spoken in the wind

my dear! empires always fall
remember when I told you
not to think about it?
these days
I easily get lost in the living room
and every day I wait for you to join reality

we still live in water

a minute of music. inside a car, we hear music driving fast through city streets in the rain. we get out of the car and hear the doors slam as the car drives away. we walk up the steps and to a building's elevator. we go up until we see the number 6174 on the door. the sound of keys turning in the lock. we enter as keys fall into a stone bowl. we open the window and listen to voicemails which are all by a single person:

I love you
how easily you forgot
now I'm alone with the spirits
I say: "I will never forget"

the dog needs attention
boiled food
monthly vaccines

I love you
how easily you forgot
now I sink into the couch
and say "I will never forget"
the African fig tree
needs to be watered three times a day

forget the dog and the fig tree
I love you
this house is too small
for all this oblivion

music. we are sitting on the balcony of the same
house. we hear the sound of nocturnal winds
blowing in a tower facing the Ocean. we hear
these words from another voicemail:

tonight I've worn this body
and these wings
they've grown larger
but one can never hear
legible sounds from the sky
but I've sat facing it
this view makes my bones
feel like bioluminescent algae
and this dawned on me:

I love the liberty in your eyes

❧ The Rain-Taxi

in the rain-taxi
majestic hawks fly towards
cliffs of solitude
when you put your head
up to its windows
you can see hummingbirds
flying in golden gardens

the rain-taxi travels along the length of the night
from rain-filled reservoirs to planets far away
to cities you want to live in
from the past to the future
treading narrow roads
by the Oceanside
when waves crash upon cement wave breakers

the rain-taxi poured from the sky
evaporated on the ground
like the heat emanating
from blades of grass at dusk
towards a moonless sky

✍ Open Horizons

the OceanDweller stands by the white poplar

everyone here has once lost something to time
each solved mystery leads us to a mystery darker than
the last
sometimes I speak to spirits
they come here longing

Jabir Ibn Hayyan[15] says that matter contains two distinct
qualities: they are either sulfurous or mercurial. he
called sulfur and mercury "poetic matter". he believed
that matter could not be organized by simple
observation, but that it needed complex equipment with
the help of which observation could become more
precise. perhaps this was the very reason why he had
many opposers, since his opposition still insisted on the
primacy of the elements such as earth, fire, water and
air. he spent his entire life relentlessly researching. he
called all matter which hovered between natural states
"hasteful" matter. they do not settle in a single form but
are constantly changing. one important application of
such "hasteful" matter was to build intergalactic
chariots. such matter could allow to escape terminal
velocity and reach open horizons

> we see the OceanCruiser from the outside. it is
> moving through stardust: these are the endless
> corridors of memory. with every birth a new
> star is born into this world and every death
> takes a star to eternity

night begins. crickets chirping to the moon. in a
room with a television buzzing. we hear this
poem from the television:

I've been staring at the sky for a while
til this moment I haven't seen a single bird
nocturnal skies have no birds
who knows
maybe one night I'll take flight from my window
to become the first nocturnal bird

to be honest when you're depressed
you're not afraid of owls or bats
or even heights

in the psychiatrist's office. by the window,
opening it only to hear the outside world
scream at the inside. closes the window. then
speaks

we had to separate like war-torn countries
there was no other way
no one was to blame
when war starts we're all to blame
she told me once
"if I die before you – which is very likely –
I'll leave my memories to you
so you can keep them safe
beside your own memories
so when you die, we can die together"

I said "do you believe we'll be reanimated with a
trumpet?"
she didn't respond

I said "reality differs from memory
memories are our instruments to battle pain
we build memories to forget reality
no matter how painful the reality
memories take root and widen past reality"

the green-purple artificial flowers were silent in the
corner of the room
like me, sorrowfully sitting on a grey bench
                    waiting

Glossary

1. The Predator of Youche is a mythical creature from the Youche region, the birthplace of Nima Yushij, the father of the Farsi free verse.
2. Mohammadi's translation of a famous verse by Nima Yushij
3. The Epipelagic layer of the Ocean is where enough sunlight exists for algae to photosynthesize.
4. Mythical marine life, mollusks with resplendent skin whose metal skeleton is revealed through their translucent flesh.
5. The coastal region of Balochistan, Pakistan.
6. Referring to Byrd Bailor's "Hawk, I'm your brother".
7. Famous line by Alfred Lord Tennyson.
8. Famous line by Dylan Thomas.
9. Famous line by Federico Garcia Lorca.
10. From Ernest Hemingway's *A Moveable Feast.*
11. "The Assyrian tree" refers to a poem written in Middle Persian.
12. Reference to Lord Byron.
13. A shrub, quite common in Iran whose scientific name is Euonymus.
14. A class of natural pigments.
15. The best-known Islamicate Alchemist.

☙ Notes

Saeed Tavanaee:

The OceanDweller began with a few marionettes, created on the long nights between 2016 and 2018 at Studio Wall. Wahid Erfanian listened to its first performances between 2016 and 2018 and provided me with much inspiration. During the Covid19 Lockdown Siroos Milani proposed a radio play based on the first chapter of *The OceanDweller*, and was the sound director for the entire multimedia program, with minimal equipment, from his small apartment in Istanbul. He is the eternal companion of *The OceanDweller*.

Khashayar Mohammadi came from the heavens, and with their incredible knowledge and expertise in poetry and translation, recreated this project once again in the English language. God knows how much I owe to them.

Last but not least, I am grateful for my mother who lived poetry to teach poetry to us, for my brother Babak who illustrated *The OceanDweller* with amazing paintings, for my sister Laleh who is my guardian angel, for my father whose smile forever illuminates my world, for uncle Hadi – the greatest writer and poet I've witnessed from closeby – and his belief in this book and all his support, for aunty Fariba who listened to every chapter of *The OceanDweller* incisively and gave her feedback and my dear poet friend, Philip Metres who read the translation and pointed out certain flaws. I am thankful for all of you.

Khashayar Mohammadi:

Great thanks to Saeed, a translator himself, who gave me space and creative freedom like no other. This project was truly exceptional, and I'll never forget the summer of working on this translation.

Several of these poems appeared in an Above/Ground chapbook of the same name. Thanks to *Periodicities* and *The Malahat Review* for publishing a few of the poems as well.

✒ About the Authors

Saeed Tavanaee Marvi is a poet and translator born in the city of Mashhad in 1983. His books include *The Woman With Chlorophylic eyes*, *Verses of Death: An Anthology of American Poetry* and a translation of Richard Brautigan's *Tokyo Montana Express*.

Khashayar "Kess" Mohammadi (They/Them) is a queer, Iranian-born, Toronto-based Poet, Writer and Translator. They were shortlisted for the 2021 Austin Clarke Poetry Prize, the 2022 Arc Poem of the Year Award, and they are the winner of the 2021 Vallum Poetry Prize. They have authored four poetry chapbooks and translated two others. Their debut poetry collection, *Me, You, Then Snow*, and their second collection, *WJD*, are both available through Gordon Hill Press.